Guns In Our Community

Protecting Yourself and Others from Gun Violence

Written and Illustrated By Robin A. Lewis

About the Author

Robin A. Lewis has been painting and drawing for many years. For the past 15 years, she has written short poems and stories. She is passionate about many things that inspire people and affect positive change. Her two children have been her inspiration for writing and becoming a published author.

Learn more about her at www.robinlewisart.com

Copyrighted Material 2022 The Writers Pub

ISBN 979-8-9870620-0-5   LOC 2022947694

Guns are Firearms

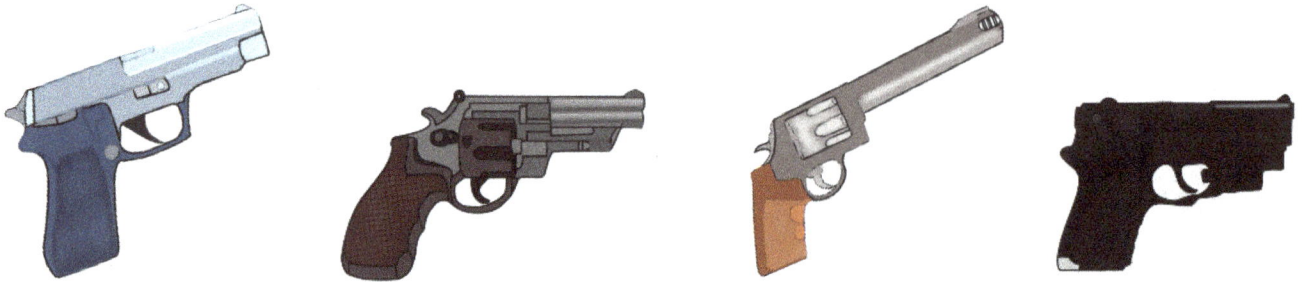

A gun is any firearm used to project or expel a particular kind of ammunition. This includes pistols, rifles, machine guns, or assault weapons. Guns come in different sizes and colors, and many of them are made differently. Guns are considered destructive weapons.

Ammunition is Bullets

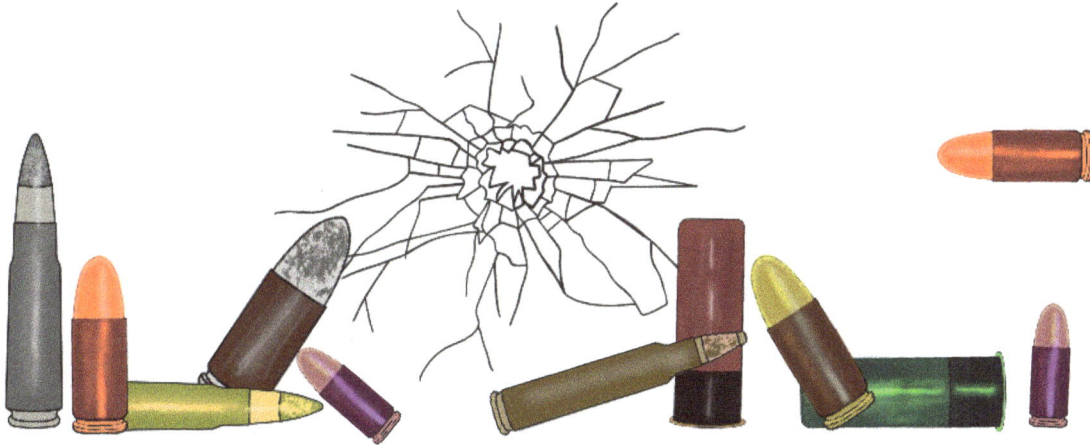

Ammunition or ammo is a type of bullet, shell, or explosive placed inside a gun. Different guns require different ammunition. Bullets come in many sizes, shapes, and colors; some are more powerful than others. They can be placed in magazines or put directly into the gun. Any bullet can be deadly when it is expelled from a gun.

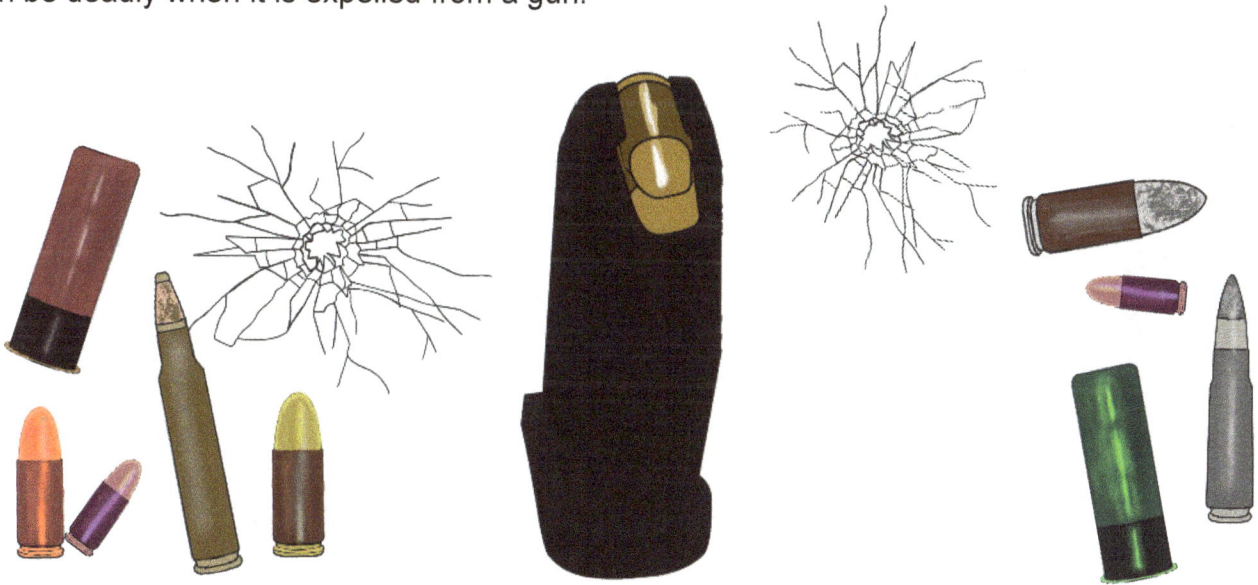

Who Usually Carry Guns

Licensed gun owners who abide by gun rules, laws, and regulations issued by the federal government can carry a gun or firearm. This would include military personnel, security personnel, and hunters.

Police
Officer

Military
Soldier

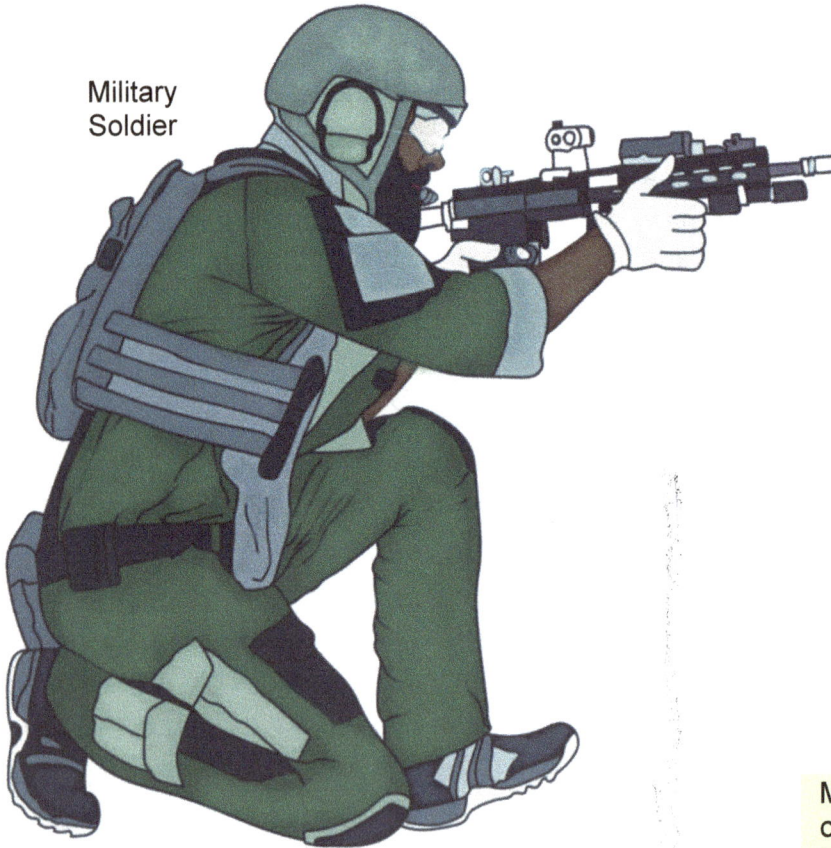

Military personnel, police, and security officers carry guns to protect civilians, government agencies, and our country.

Regular civilians make up the majority of individuals that own or carry guns. A civilian may carry a firearm if they can legally own one. These people should be accountable for their guns, and they are more likely to have trained in using their weapons and have been educated on gun safety, gun rules, and gun regulations. It is a big responsibility to be a gun owner.

Hunter

Civilian

A person of any gender can legally own a gun.

Hunters use guns to capture or kill wild animals for food or sport.

Who Should Not Have a Gun

People who should not have a gun include unstable people who lack the ability to make rational decisions when using a gun. People that purposely use guns for violent acts and criminal activity on innocent people. Children, babies, teenagers, and other people who can not legally carry or use a firearm. These people should not have access to a gun or have one in their possession at any time.

Teenager

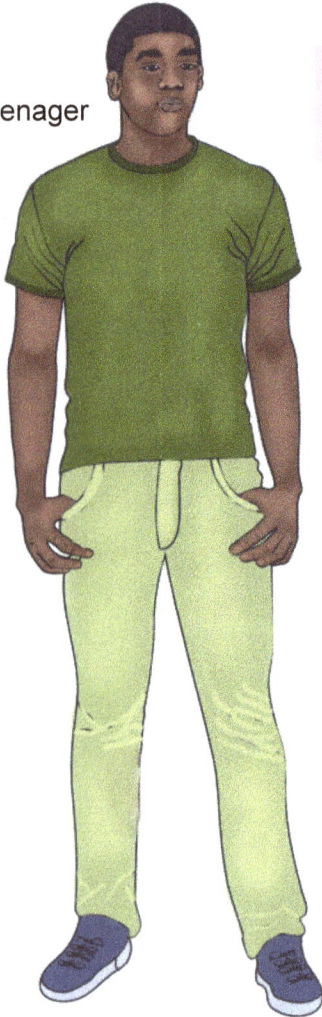

Babies, children, and teenagers cannot be gun owners.

Child

Criminal or Thief

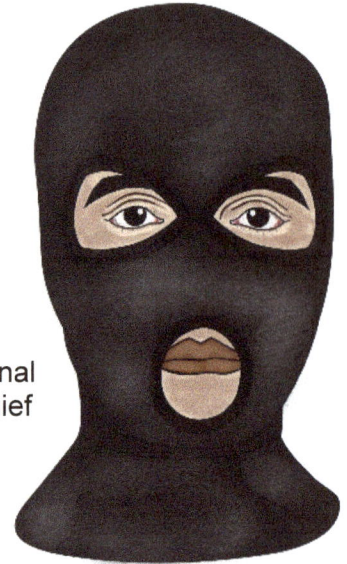

People that use guns purposely to commit crimes and gun violence should not have a gun.

Baby

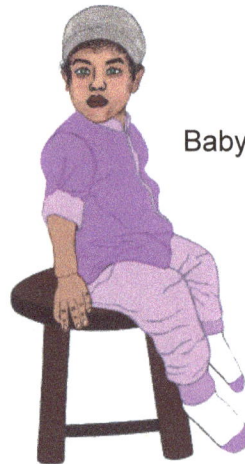

Children will Learn

Children will learn about guns at some point in their childhood from their parents, friends, video games, or the internet, and because they do not understand how dangerous guns are, it is never too early to teach them the difference between a real and a fake gun. It is also important to teach them about gun safety and what they can do if they are caught in gunfire.

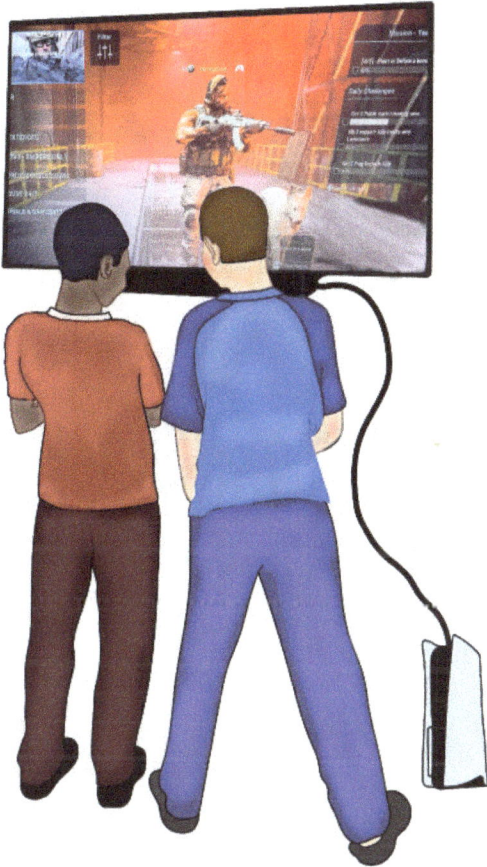

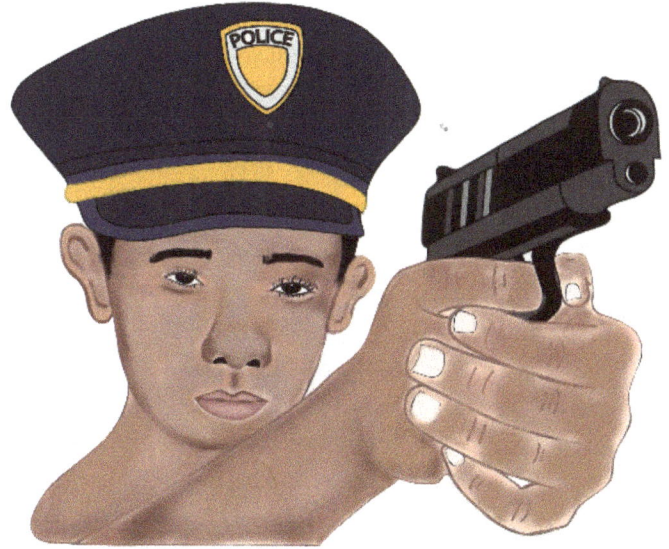

Children as young as 3 years old are often dressed in costumes imitating police officers, cowboys, or characters that carry toy guns or assault weapons.

Some children are fascinated by guns because many play video games using handguns and assault weapons. They may also be introduced to them innocently by people; this includes recreational and toy guns like the ones pictured right.

Paper Gun

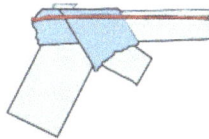

BB Gun

Air Gun

Fake or Toy Gun

Water Gun

Guns Safety In The Home

Thousands of children die from guns in the home every year, and many are hurt or left with permanent injuries. Guns should never be left under car seats, pillows, or on tables. People who own guns are responsible for keeping their weapons locked up, safe, and out of the hands of unauthorized users, especially children.

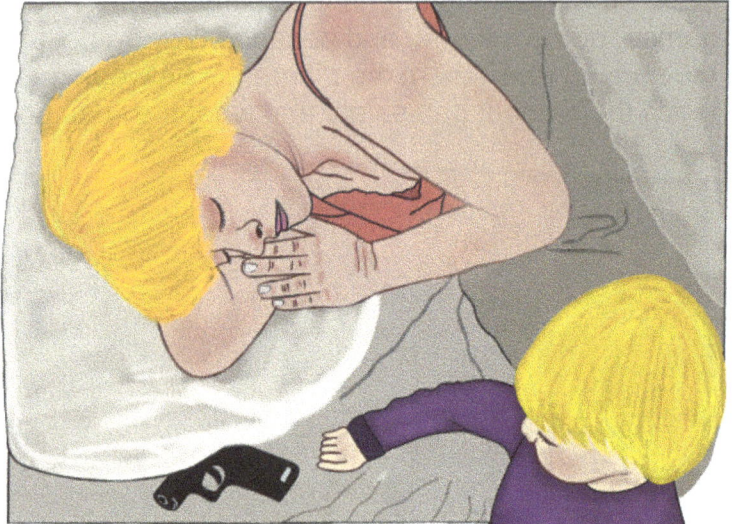

Guns in the home are the number one cause of death by suicide among young children, this includes both accidental and intentional suicides.

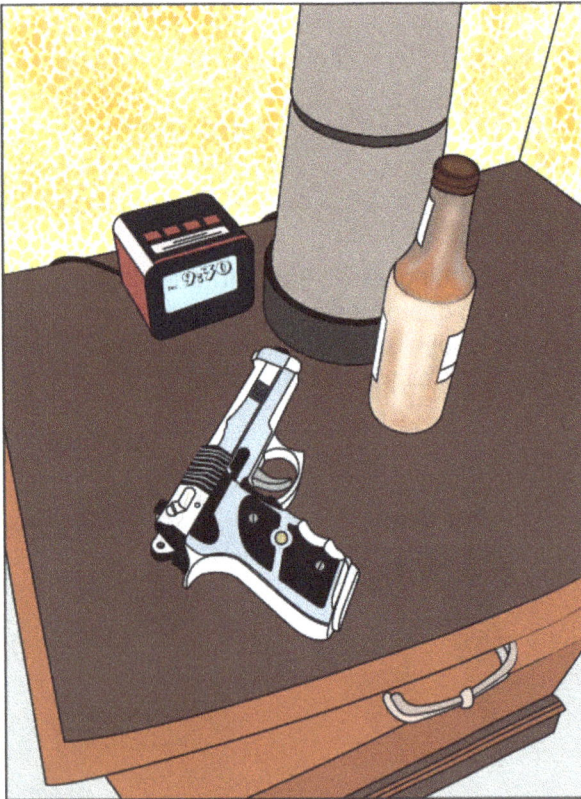

Guns should never be left anywhere loaded or unloaded for children and other people to access.

Guns Safety

Guns in the home, office, business, and other establishments should be locked in a safe, gun box, or gun cabinet, away from children and out of the way of other people. Ammunition should be locked away and stored securely, separately from the gun. Gun shops carry lock boxes and safes for gun owners. This can keep guns away from unauthorized people.

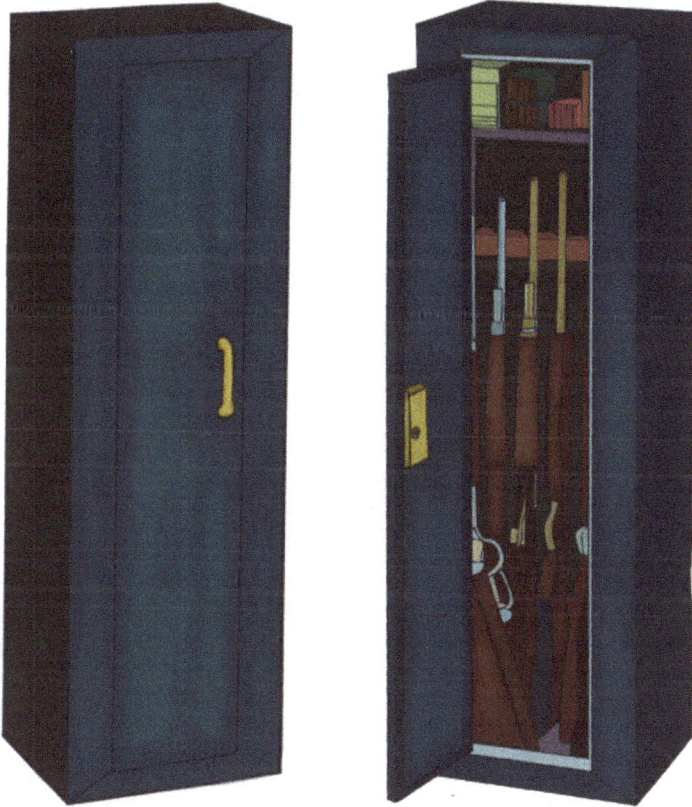

Guns should be stored with a lock and key, out of sight. If a gun falls into a child's hand, the gun owner may be penalized.

In The Wrong Hands

Guns are everywhere, and they are often in the hands of people who abuse them and use them to hurt others. Many firearms are often found by hundreds of children in the home who injure or kill themselves every year. In many cases, the caregiver is also present during the incident. These are some ways that guns may get into the hands of unauthorized people.

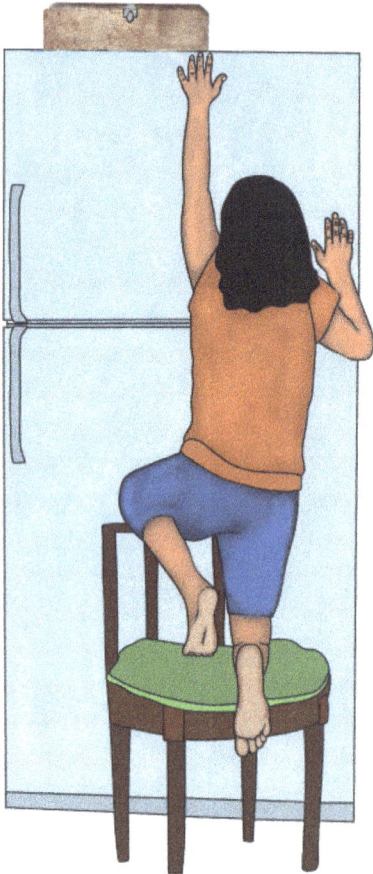

Guns in The Wrong Hands

- stolen in robberies or thefts
- stolen out of vehicles
- bought from legal or illegal gun dealers
- made from gun parts
- found by adults and children
- easily accessible in the home

Small children can grab a loaded gun in a few seconds and discharge it, even if you are nearby.

Guns hidden in high places may still be dangerous, especially if they are placed in containers that can easily be opened by curious children.

Unauthorized people may still purchase a gun without questions since background checks in many states are not required. This includes criminals and people that are prohibited from buying a gun. When a firearm is purchased from a licensed dealer, the sale identifies the seller and the buyer, making the buyer responsible for the weapon. While the dealer retains sale information, only 5 states are required to report these sales to law enforcement. These guns include rifles and assault weapons.

Finding A Gun

Guns are often discarded in trash cans, rivers, and other places, which is why many of them end up in the wrong hands. If you find a gun, do not touch it, the gun may have been used in a crime, or you could seriously injure or kill yourself or someone else. Always assume that guns are loaded.

Call 911 and report the lost gun. Give them a description of the gun and where it was found.

Gun in the trash can

Tell an adult. This may be a parent, guardian, teacher, neighbor, or law enforcement officer.

Reporting a lost or stolen gun may save a life by keeping the gun out of the wrong hands.

People with guns in their possession

Some people think it is cool to carry a gun; it may be a friend or someone you don't know. If you are in a situation where the people you are with are handling or using a gun, do not stay around them. Talk to an adult immediately about the incident. Always assume that a gun is loaded and that it can injure or kill someone. If you are with people that have a gun and a crime is committed, you may be arrested and placed in jail for a long time.

GUNS ARE NOT TOYS

HE HAS A GUN ITS COOL MAN

I'M NOT COMFORTABLE WITH THIS SOMEBODY COULD GET HURT

gun in bag

Never take guns to school, even if it is a fake gun. Someone could get hurt or killed, mistaking a fake gun for a real one.

CALL 911

LEAVE THE AREA

CALL MY DAD

If you see Something Say Something

Do not feel pressured to participate or stay around people that have guns. Talk to someone that you trust when you feel safe.

Gun Violence

Gun violence is a violent act committed by the use of a gun. Over 85,000 people are injured by gun violence each year, with more than 32,000 dying. Hospital injuries, increased police enforcement, crime, and the rise in death rates every year are the results of gun violence.

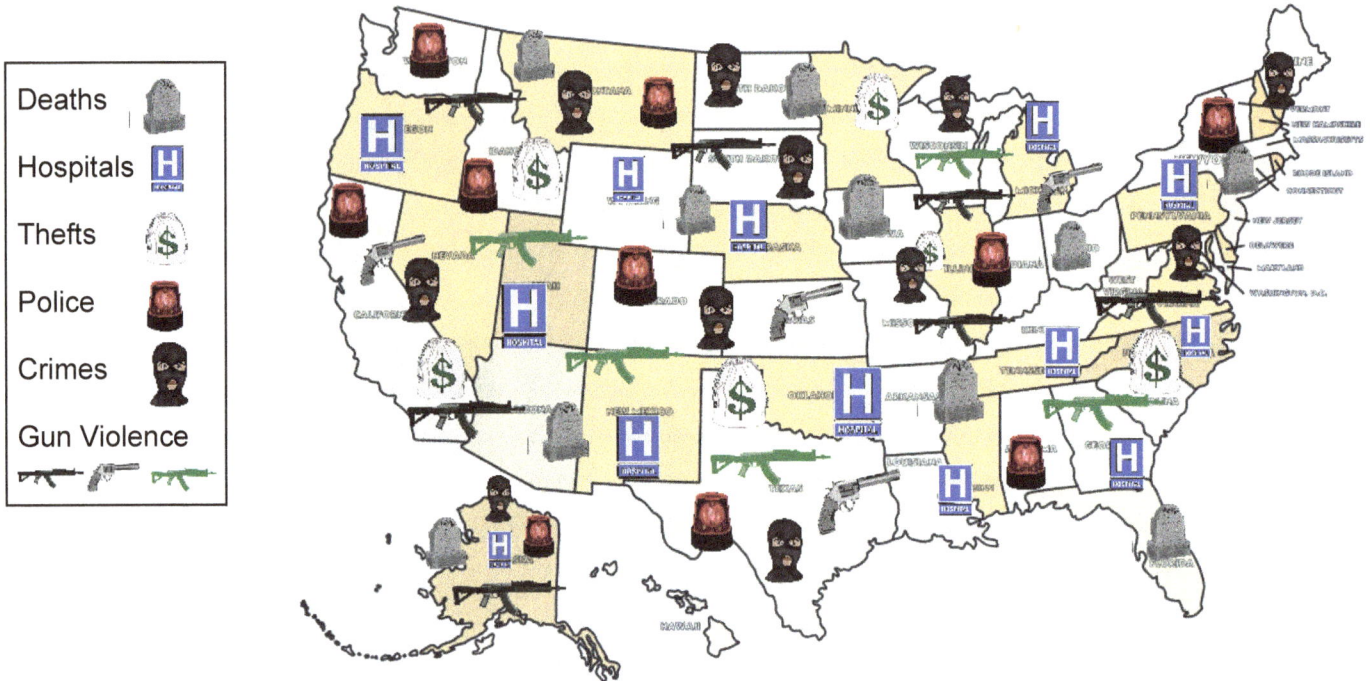

Deaths
Hospitals
Thefts
Police
Crimes
Gun Violence

Gun violence in the community occurs mainly in cities

Types Of Gun Violence

- homicide and violent crimes
- assault with a gun
- mass shootings
- unintentional death or injury
- domestic violence with a gun
- suicide or attempted suicide

Many things can promote or lead to gun violence. A minor disagreement can escalate, leading to gunfire that may injure or kill innocent people. In today's society, gun violence can happen anywhere at any time, including areas that have never had gun violence before. Gun violence can happen at a grocery store, school, baseball game, party, park, church, movie theater, or anywhere else.

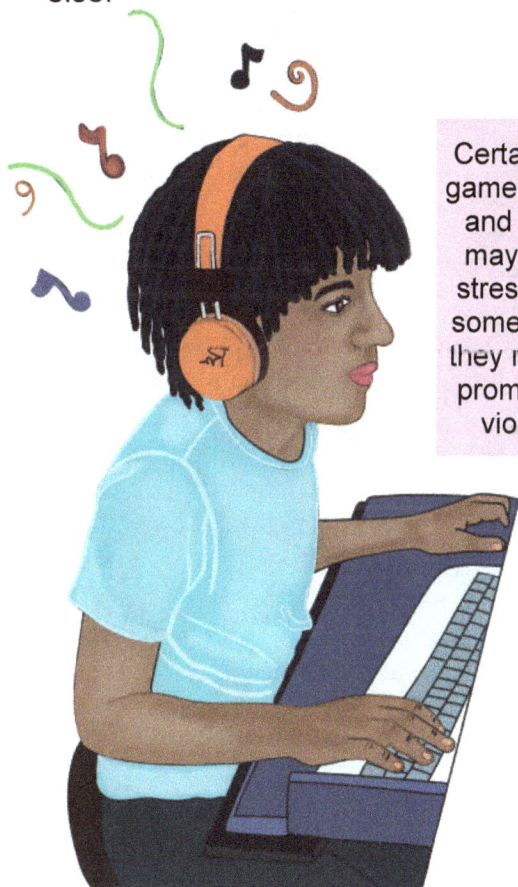

Things that may contribute to gun violence

Jealousy	Peer Pressure
Anger	Financial Stress
Bullying	Homelessness
Fear	Threats
Depression	Mental Illness
Hate	Poverty

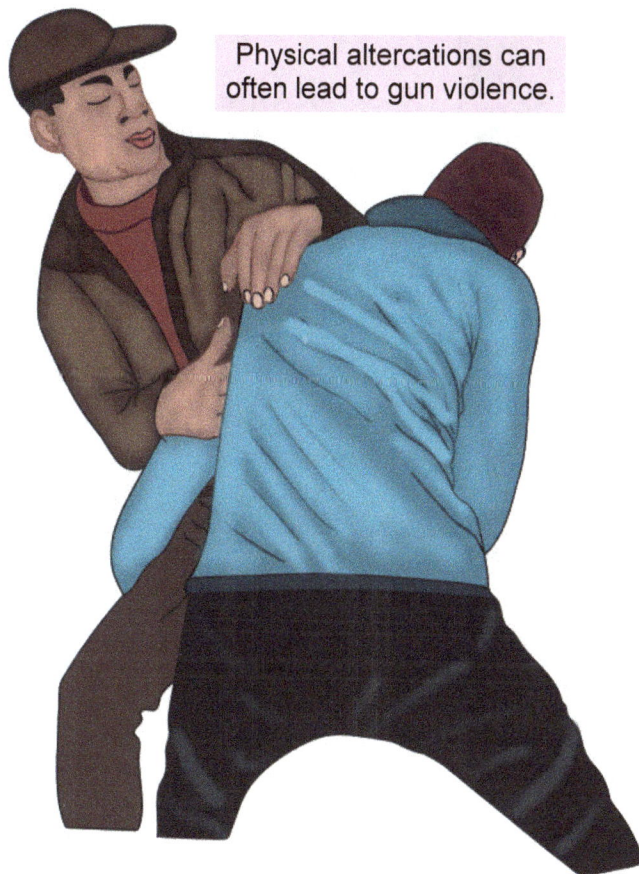

Certain video games, music, and movies may relieve stress, but in some people, they may also promote gun violence.

Physical altercations can often lead to gun violence.

Guns in The Community

In 2022, in the United States, firearms became the leading cause of death in children and teens between the ages of 1-18. Young children have accidentally accessed guns in their homes or elsewhere and have died by suicide. Many teenagers have witnessed the death of a friend or lost their own lives by gunfire in inner city communities. If you have experienced gun violence, you are not alone.

These scenes have become routine for many neighborhoods in inner cities in the United States.

Every year, over 117,000 people in America are injured, killed, or die by suicide from gunshots. This includes more than 8,000 children who are shot yearly, and many of them die from their injuries. Children who do survive often suffer a lifetime of disabilities and medical conditions that lead into their adult lives.

Over 300 people are shot each day, making the hospital cost related to gun injuries more than 1 billion dollars a year.

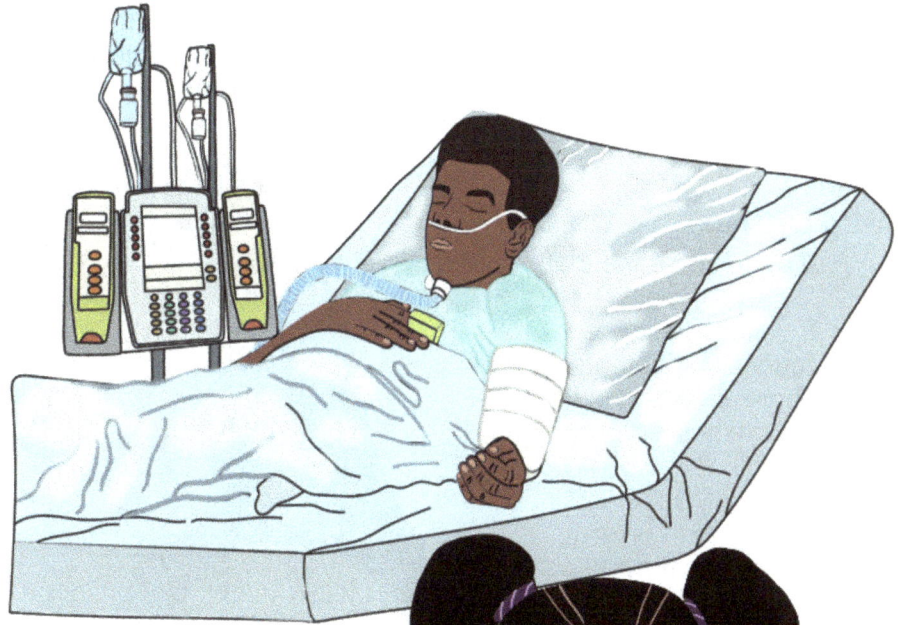

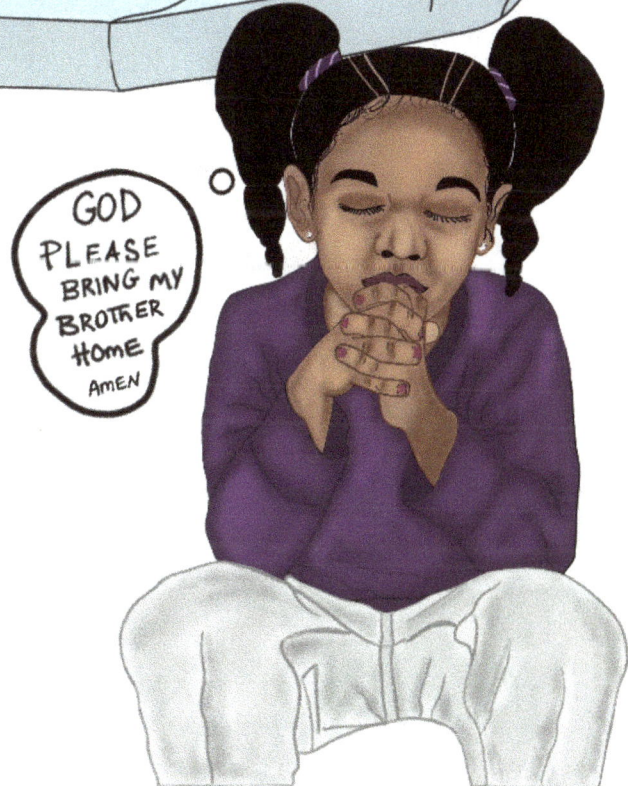

People Hurt Other People

Some people use guns to hurt others. They may be angry, confused, or having a mental health crisis. People may find other reasons to commit a violent act to injure or kill someone with a gun, but they should never be used, no matter the situation.

It's OK NOT To Be OK

- Talk to someone that you trust
- Ask for help from counselors, parents, teachers, and friends
- Call the crisis hotline in your area if you feel like hurting yourself or someone else
- Hospitals may also assist with crisis intervention

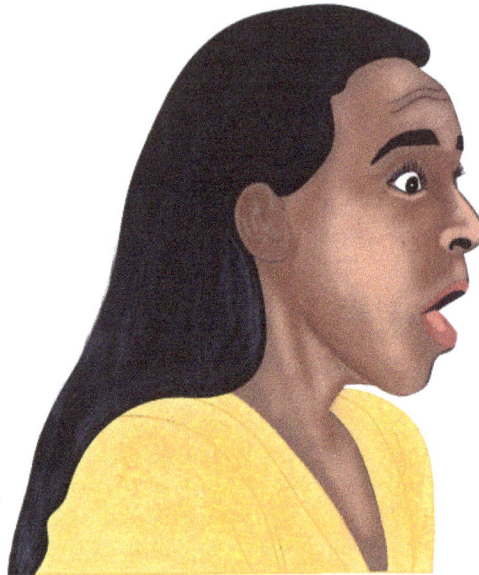

GIVE UP THE MONEY

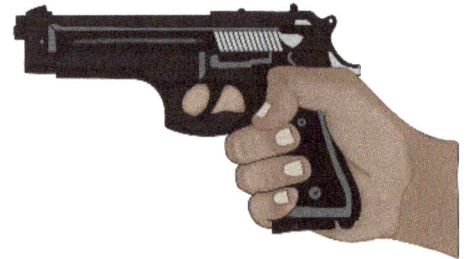

If you are in a situation involving a gun, try to stay as calm as possible.

GUN VIOLENCE HURTS EVERYONE, NO MATTER WHAT AGE THEY ARE

Bullets and Gunfire

People who survive after being shot may have to live their lives differently, and they may lose their ability to walk, talk and care for themselves independently. The damage from gunfire often leaves permanent and life changing injuries and trauma. We should be patient with people who are recovering from gunshot injuries because their new way of life may be challenging for them.

Many people must change their daily activities to accommodate their new medical conditions.

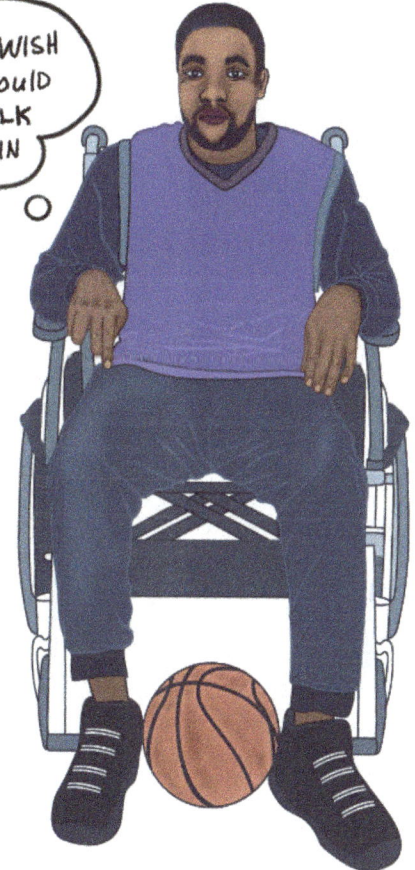

Mass Shootings

Mass shootings are crimes committed with a gun that kills 4 or more people. These shootings are done with the intent to injure or kill people. An active shooter is a person that is firing a gun. Active shooters can be anyone.

Pulse Night Club

On June 16th, 2016, in Orlando, Florida, Omar Matten age 29, opened fire in one of Orlando's biggest nightclubs called "Pulse". This mass shooting took the lives of 50 people and wounded 53.

Loved ones and friends gathered for memorial services. across the country.

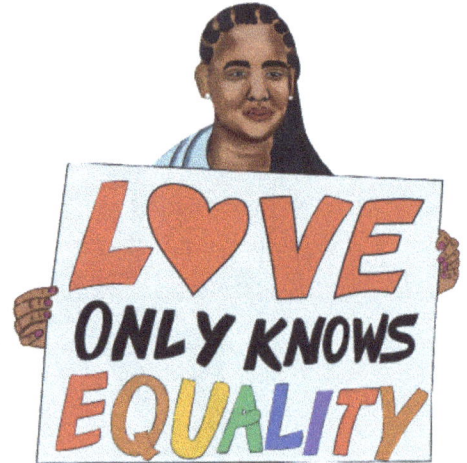

First Baptist Church

On November 5th 2017, 24 year old David Katz entered the First Baptist Church in Sutherland Springs, Texas. He opened fire, killing 26 people and wounding 22. This is the deadliest shooting for a place of worship in US history.

A rose was placed on a chair for each victim during a memorial service at the First Baptist Church.

Active shooters may target specific groups of people based on their race, age, nationality, sexual gender, or religion. Shooters may find many other reasons to target an individual or group of people.

Virginia Tech University

On April 6th 2007, 23 year old Seung-Hui Cho opened fire at Virginia Tech University in Blacksburg, Virginia. 32 people were killed, and 17 people were wounded.

Students embrace each other at a memorial service for VA Tech victims.

Music Festival

On October 1st 2017, in Las Vegas, Nevada, 64 year old Stephen Paddock opened fire on a crowd attending the Route 91 Music Festival. He shot and killed 60 people and injured over 400 from his 32nd floor hotel suite. This is the deadliest mass shooting in US history.

58 crosses were left for the victims of The Route 91 Festival.

Protesters in Florida after school shooting

Robb Elementary School

On May 24, 2022, in Uvalde, Texas, 18 year old Salvador Ramos opened fire inside Robb Elementary School. He fatally killed 19 students and 2 teachers. Many others were wounded.

Mass shootings are happening more and more around the country.

Families gathered for a memorial of their loved ones.

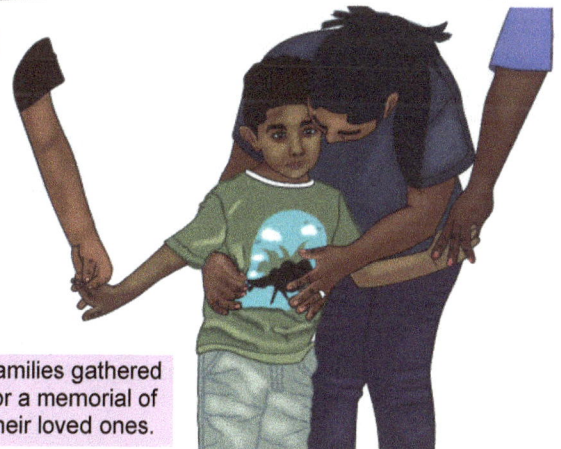

Bullets and Gunfire

Since gunfire can happen at any time, you may be in a place where someone starts shooting. This could be a shopping mall, playground, school, or anywhere. Take precautions so that you do not get injured or killed. When bullets are expelled from a gun, they can go through doors, walls, windows, and anywhere else, including you.

#1 Find a safe place to hide where bullets cannot reach you.

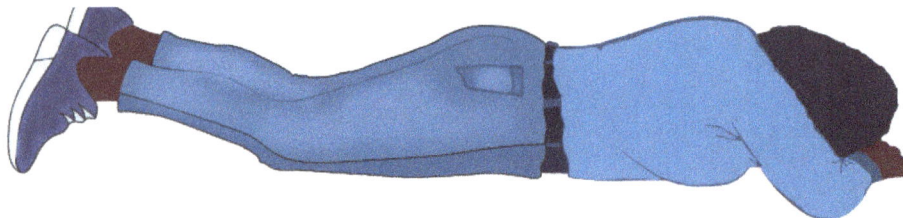

#2 Stop and lay flat on the ground if you cannot leave the area immediately. This may prevent you from getting hit by a flying bullet.

Guns do not shoot themselves; people shoot them. Being quiet may save your life if someone is looking to hurt you. Call for help when you feel safe to let people know where you are. You may save your life or another person's by calling for help.

#3 Be quiet until help comes. Being silent may save your life.

#4 If you do not feel safe talking on your phone, texting may be a safer way to communicate. Text 911 for help.

911

NOT ONE MORE

23

The Effects of Gun Violence on Children

In some communities, guns are easily accessible to anyone, including children. These children experience gun violence routinely and suffer distress from witnessing or hearing gunshots. This area has lower household incomes and employment rates, fewer educational resources, and a lack of state funding. Many people in these communities do not report crimes for fear of retaliation or because they do not trust law enforcement. Gun violence severely affects children's growth and development because it is heavily promoted in these communities.

Children and Teens

- Drop out of school
- Fail in school
- May demonstrate violent or negative behaviors
- Become antisocial, distant, and act aggressive or angry
- May feel the need to carry a gun for protection
- Use alcohol, drugs, or tobacco
- may feel sad and depressed
- may develop ADHD and anxiety
- Develop health issues over time as they get older

BEER

F

Due to gun violence, children are often left without a parent, caregiver, sibling, loved one, or friend. They may need counseling and assistance until they reach adulthood. Some children, unfortunately, end up in foster care because they no longer have a caregiver at home. These significant changes can leave children feeling abandoned, stressed out, and depressed for a long time.

A sudden change in circumstances may be traumatizing for some children.

Candlelight vigils are held daily across the US to honor loved ones and friends who have died from gun violence .

Gun Violence in the Community

Gun violence affects everyone in the community. People often feel unsafe and afraid. Children may be afraid to play outside, decreasing socialization and increasing isolation. Doing everyday things often becomes a challenge. The trauma from gun violence, injury, or death may be slow or no recovery. The lives of many people are changed forever.

Financial, medical, and burial expenses for survivors can be very stressful.

The community, loved ones, and friends suffer significant losses from gun violence.
Gun violence hurts everyone.

FOR SALE

202-889-1726

POLICE LINE DO NOT CROSS

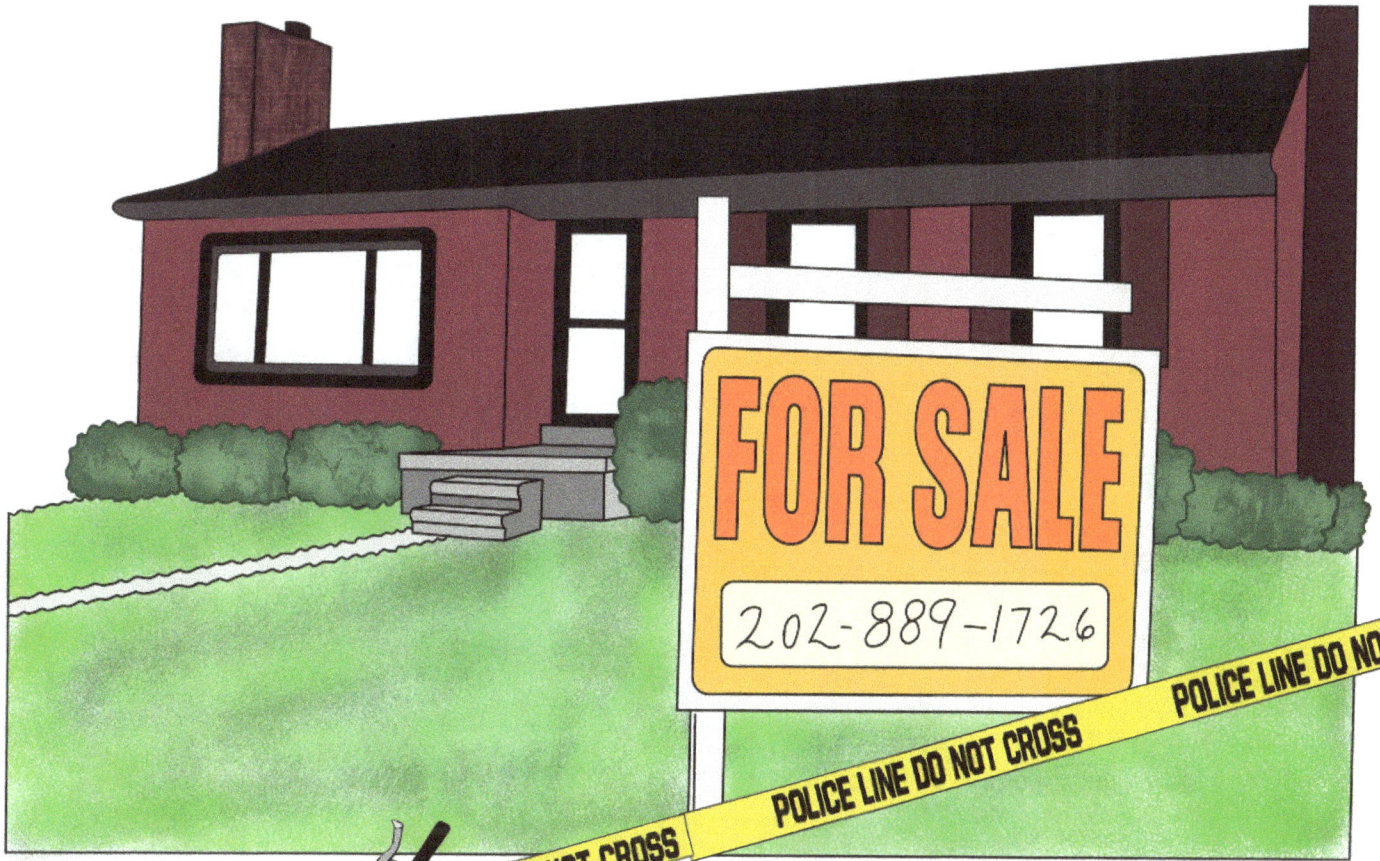

Housing value in these areas decrease, and there may be very few retail stores.

We all need to work together to end gun violence. Everyone has the right to be safe in their neighborhood.

Preventing Gun Violence in The Community

Communities are working hard to prevent gun violence in their neighborhoods. Community leaders are implementing more programs and resources to keep young people educated and occupied in healthy things to help them make the best choices.

Actions the Community May Take

- Universal Background checks for people purchasing guns
- Increase school and neighborhood security
- Ban assault weapons
- Increase community programs resources
- Encourage parents to discuss gun violence with their children and teens
- Promote gun safety in and out of the home
- Buyback guns in the community
- Community events that educate and encourage youth to put guns down
- Promote gun safety in and out of the home
- Child safety features for all firearms

Buyback Guns
Stop the Violence

No Questions Asked
Cash Paid

May 13th 3-10 pm

STOP GUN VIOLENCE

ASSAULT WEAPONS

Put Da Gunz Down

COMMUNITY CENTER

POLICE

You Can Help to prevent Gun Violence

You can help promote gun safety and help to end gun violence by deciding not to use a gun to harm another person. We all need help sometimes; ask for help from a parent, teacher, counselor, or another adult. They may help solve problems and conflicts. We all need to work together to end gun violence. Everyone has the right to live, work and play without fearing gun violence in their community.

How Children and Teens Can Help

- Assume all guns are loaded, Do not use or handle guns
- Be mindful of the people you hang with
- Avoid places where guns are being used
- Let people know where you are
- Talk and solve problems together
- Report bullying and abuse to an adult
- Never aim a gun at anyone, even a toy gun
- Tell someone if you feel depressed or suicidal
- Report a lost or stolen gun
- Report juveniles and unauthorized gun users

Always remember the people you love.

www.ingramcontent.com/pod-product-compliance
Lightning Source LLC
Chambersburg PA
CBHW080429030426
42335CB00020B/2652